The Eight Aspects of God

A Pathway to Bliss

Ruthie Stender

Published 2012
Printed in the United States of America
ISBN: 978-0-9885345-0-6
Library of Congress Control Number: 2012920370

HenOli Press
Seattle, WA 98103
henolipress@gmail.com

To my mom.

"May the long time sun shine upon you.
All love surround you.
And the pure light within you guide your
way on."

—*Snatum Kuar*, *"Long Time Sun"*
from her album Grace

Contents ∞

Introduction

∞

It is through my work as an energy medicine practitioner that I learned about the body's energy centers, called chakras, and through my studies of yoga and meditation that I came upon the *eight aspects of God*. Aligning the God aspects—peace, wisdom, power, love, calmness, light, sound, and bliss—to a specific chakra gave me a framework, a structure, that made practical sense to me, furthering my understanding of how the body and mind integrate with spirit. This new roadmap felt like an effective strategy for teaching others about the body's energy system while at the same time exploring a new path toward spiritual development.

If we believe that the body's job is to serve the spirit, it makes sense that we work to understand how the body, mind, and spirit are connected in order to help ourselves. The God aspects—more specifically, living in alignment with them—is a way to connect mind, body, and spirit by way of the energy centers. This approach to healing becomes easy, and keeps us interested and wanting more, because the aspects, in and of themselves, are things we all strive for in the first place. Who doesn't want more peace, wisdom, love, or bliss? We all do! Taking steps to invite these aspects into your life automatically improves your health because of their direct link to the energy centers. Any issue that shows up in physical form can be traced back to an energy center in the body, and, ultimately, a missing *aspect* in your life.

This book is about self-discovery, self-healing, and self-empowerment. It was birthed from a series of articles that I wrote for my column, "Chakra Talk," in *New Spirit Journal,* a Seattle-based newspaper. Much of the content for the articles was borrowed from my forthcoming book, *It's Not About You,* which gets more involved in the self-discovery process by using exercises to determine highs and lows in the energy body and offering suggestions on how to correct those imbalances.

The idea to create a shorter book came from my desire to share those articles, as a whole, with my clients and students. Instead of going to the local copy center to whip up a handful of copies to take with me on the go (which is what I was planning to do!), my writing coach suggested that I make an e-book and smaller print version as I work to complete the larger book. This book is based on the core principles of the soon-to-be-released larger book, *It's Not About You.*

The reason it's so important for me to share my knowledge about the body's innate ability to heal itself is that it comes from my own personal experience. Finding energy medicine changed—and then saved—my life and ultimately brought me closer to my own God aspects, my soul, along the way. I got very ill and became vulnerable to the actions and behaviors of others when I separated from my true soul self. I lost my sense of worth, personal power, and self-love. I was taking what others did personally, as if they were doing "it" to me. Now that I'm on the other side of this experience, I find myself in a spiritually centered space where I feel a true connection, a genuine kinship, with others. I see that others are doing what they do because of where they are on their own path. Instead of holding expectations and judgments, I feel a sense of compassion and understanding toward people.

I believe that sharing what I know will help others. And that's the bottom line for why I'm writing this book. I believe that all illness stems from our separation from spirit. My desire is to offer you a roadmap as you make your way home back to spirit—perhaps making your journey a little less bumpy than mine has been. This little book holds gems to help you get a little closer to your own God aspects. My hope is that it really will help you in this way.

I believe that what makes us feel connected as human beings is that we all possess, or at least want to posses, these God aspects. What makes us different is the degree to which we each express, or don't express, them. What brings us closer together is seeing our differences without wanting to change one another, understanding that each of us is on our own journey home, our own path toward our own unique expression of God. My intention is to help remove the ignorance, the lack of understanding, that divides us—not just from our own souls, but each other's.

Chapter 1:

An Overview of The Eight Aspects of God

There's a magnificent structure of energy centers (chakras) throughout and around our bodies that governs every facet of our lives. The word *chakra* comes from Sanskrit, one of the ancient languages of India, and is commonly referred to in the practices of yoga and meditation.

There are seven major chakras, and each receives and transmits life force energy. When understood, they can also act as guideposts on our journey through life. It is believed that our bodies have thousands of chakras, but if we learn to work with the seven primary ones, the others—through the act of entrainment—vibrate to the healthier frequency of those primary seven.

The first six chakras align with and run the length of the spine—starting at the base, at the coccyx, and ending at the medulla, at the lower back of the skull in the area of the occipital ridge. The medulla region is considered to be the negative pole of the sixth chakra; its positive counterpoint is located at the point between the eyebrows, also known as the third eye. The seventh, and final, major chakra is located at the top of the head and is called the crown chakra.

Paramhansa Yogananda, the great yogi who brought yoga to the west in the 1920s, teaches us that there are eight aspects of God: peace, wisdom, power, love, calmness, sound, light, and joy (or bliss). When we marry these eight aspects with the major chakras, we are given an easy roadmap to help us balance our energy body.

Starting with the first chakra and going all the way up to the seventh, the aspects align like this:

Chakra 1, the root chakra: peace
Chakra 2, the sacral chakra: wisdom
Chakra 3, the navel chakra: power
Chakra 4, the heart chakra: love
Chakra 5, the throat chakra: calmness
Chakra 6, the third eye chakra: light (as in *to see the light*) and sound
Chakra 7, the crown chakra: bliss

The fact is, whether you know anything about the chakras or not, if you work to bring these eight aspects into your life, you will experience greater health and happiness. This is not so dissimilar from taking care of your car. You don't need to know the ins and outs of what makes your car run, but you do need to know what to do to ensure that your car operates over the long term. You know it needs gas, certain fluids, and the occasional tune-up. The same holds true for the body's energy centers. Integrating these eight aspects into your life makes you idle better, helps you to navigate through life's obstacles with ease, and assists you in finding a new route when you're confronted with a detour in the course of your journey.

I like to say that this approach induces healing "auto-magically," because we experience improved health and wellness on all levels when we embrace these positive qualities.

❋ Peace is the key aspect of the first chakra. We lose our sense of peace for many reasons, but the biggest reason is that we have lost our footing, or feel abandoned or neglected—that we don't trust life to take care of us. The root chakra thrives when we have feelings of safety, belonging, security, and peace within our environment.

❋ Wisdom is the key aspect of the second chakra, which is located a few inches above the pubic bone. To create healthy relationships and unleash hidden talents naturally and intuitively, we must draw on our deepest knowing—our soul's wisdom. By drawing on ancient wisdom, found deep within every part of your being, your future unfolds in perfect alignment with your purpose; magically, colorful people, things, and experiences manifest in your life and the lives of those around you.

✻ Power—more specifically, personal power—is the key aspect of the third chakra. When we lose our power, we are vulnerable to falling into the role of "victim." Of all the chakras, this third energy center takes the biggest hit if we feel personally violated because of its location: right in our gut, near the navel and solar plexus. Because this is the power center, if we can learn to harness and control our personal power we are far less likely to be affected by what other people do.

✻ Love is the key aspect of the fourth chakra, located at our heart center, and can be defined as devotion. When we devote time in meditation, for example, we are in the critical mode of reciprocity. We are honoring our relationship with God by giving ourselves over in devotion while in our sacred place of stillness. And there is no greater love to be received than that which we are given during states of expansion.

❋ Calmness is the key aspect of the fifth chakra, the throat chakra. Speaking our truth sometimes makes us feel self-conscious. If we can learn to speak it joyfully, and from the heart, we realize that the authentic joy we hear is the voice of God. Therefore, one cannot fake joy. A calm heart induces joy. A calm voice allows the joy to sparkle.

❋ Light and sound are the two aspects of the sixth chakra, the third eye chakra—specifically, light, as seen in your mind's eye during higher states of consciousness, and sound, as in the cosmic vibration of aum (om). When we sit in stillness and listen (sound) for guidance from a higher source, we gain clarity (light) in our purpose, our vision. We *see the light.*

❋ Bliss is the ultimate state of joy and the key aspect of the seventh chakra, the crown chakra. Having a spiritual practice is the cornerstone of keeping the other chakras united. When we devote time to commune with Spirit on a regular basis, we find joy—bliss—in all areas of life.

Yoga and meditation are two powerful ways to invite the eight aspects into your life and to integrate the chakras as a whole system. Yoga is not about how flexible you are but about finding union with a higher source, a higher awareness. These *God aspects* are the path to finding balance and wellness on all levels—mind, body, and spirit.

Chapter 2
Peace

The first of the seven major chakras is the root chakra. Located at the base of the spine, it's also sometimes referred to as the base chakra. Each chakra has a connection to one of the four elements—earth, water, fire, or air—and the root chakra's element is earth. Because of the root chakra's earthly connection, it is especially sensitive to—and literally influenced by—our physical environment. The notion of being "rooted" or "grounded" comes from our understanding of this chakra.

The more grounded we are, the less likely we are to be influenced by negative or toxic energy in certain situations. But what does *being grounded* really mean? To be grounded means to feel safe and secure within your environment. Feeling secure cultivates a sense of peace. Peace is the absence of worry, judgment, fear, anger, or anything that puts you on guard or makes you question your place. Each chakra has negative and positive aspects, and peace is the key aspect of the root chakra. A peaceful environment keeps your first chakra balanced.

The two most important things you can do for the root chakra are: (1) create a positive and peaceful environment; and (2) learn some tools that will help you stay grounded when the occasional storm hits.

Who is Most Vulnerable to the Energy in Their Environment?

❋ Workers in the healthcare industry, because they are around people with a variety of health issues all day. Energy workers are even more at risk because many are empathic; they literally feel energy as they integrate with someone else's energy field, putting them at risk of absorbing unhealthy energy if they are not grounded.

❋ People unaware of the energetic connections around them. You might not consider that the chaotic energy being put off by your toxic coworker is what is causing your arrhythmia, or that your unhealthy roommate or partner is what is causing your migraines.

❋ Children. Children are highly sensitive to their surroundings; they learn to entrain to their various environments as a matter of course. We were all children at one time. Think about how you entrained to your own environment as a child, and about how many years you've spent absorbing toxic energy because you never learned otherwise.

Ways to Achieve a Healthy Root Chakra and Positive Environment

Exercise, mineral salt baths, detoxifying diets, and yogic and meditation practices involving bandhas, mudras, and breathing techniques are all ways to clear and protect the root chakra, but these are the three tools I most often share with people and rely on myself:

1) Psychic Protection and Space Clearing. Just like brushing your teeth, psychic protection and space clearing should become a habit for everyone. These practices protect and clear both your personal and physical environments. Imagine a golden sphere of light around you.

See this layer of protection as cosmic light, God, Spirit, or whatever image induces a strong sense of security for you. I use love because I believe nothing is stronger than love. Anything that doesn't serve you cannot penetrate this layer of protection. Learn how to burn sage (smudge) to clear negative energy from your physical space. Smudge when you sweep the floor, clean the fridge, or de-clutter your office; make it a routine practice. Afterward, to hold the positive energy in, wrap the space with your sphere and avoid allowing negative energies to enter it as much as possible.

2) Full Yogic Breath. The secret to getting centered—here, now, fast—is proper breathing. The yogic breath uses the full capacity of your lungs, clearing toxins and oxygenating the blood. Before you try it, relax and place your hands on your torso to notice how your body moves when you breathe.

Now breathe in, contracting your diaphragm muscle (located at the bottom of the lungs). Focus on pulling the breath down into the lowest part of your lungs. Gradually allow your ribs to flare to the sides as the breath fills the middle part of your lungs. Finally, allow the breath to fill your upper lungs as you feel your chest expand. Exhale in reverse, releasing air from the upper, then middle, then lower part of each lung. Do this through your nose if possible. If you feel light-headed, stop. While practicing, imagine roots growing from your feet and reaching into the earth. Inhale, drawing the earth's energy up and through your spine. Exhale, relaxing into your spine as your roots reach deep into the earth. Practicing outside under a tree is even better!

> *Tip:* Go online and look up images of the lungs and diaphragm. Study the diaphragm muscle to see its shape and how it works. Visualize the action of the diaphragm and lungs while practicing the full yogic breath.

3) **Drumming.** Drumming is an innate part of who you are. You heard the first rhythms of drumming in your mother's womb. Her heartbeat was your first introduction to the sounds of your new life on earth. This is partly why drumming is so grounding yet meditative; it engenders feelings of that safe haven of peace within the womb. Kids love drumming, most likely because they're not too far removed from that maternal experience. Moving to the beat—stomping, dancing, and jumping—gets you grounded. And as an added bonus, the good vibrations clear out any bad energy in the environment.

"Environment is stronger than will power. If you want to be spiritual, seek good company and don't mix with those whose bad habits may wrongly influence you. Be always with people who inspire you; surround yourself with people who lift you up."

—*Paramhansa Yogananda*

Work to create a healthy environment when you're feeling good! It's easier to devise a plan as a preventative measure rather than in reaction to negative or toxic energy. Not only is it easier to devise a plan when you're not under stress or in the midst of suffering, your good energy will attract positive people to you, helping you build a supportive, healthy, nurturing community.

Chapter 3
Wisdom

The second of the seven major chakras is the sacral chakra, which is located just above the pubic bone, several inches below the navel. The second chakra is directly associated with birthing new life—literally, but also symbolically, as it is the center of awakening and creating skills and talents. Creativity is not just about *creating art;* it also has to do with being creative in your relationships with people and things like jobs and finances.

To have positive relationships and maximize creative expression, we must follow our inner guidance, our soul's wisdom. We do that by learning about what governs the second chakra. The sacral chakra is connected to water.

Water is fluid, dynamic, and needs to flow—otherwise it becomes stagnant. Similarly, it's important to keep an open, flowing creative channel in your life to stave off rigidity and atrophy. Creativity is essential for inviting in, and staying connected to, your deep inner wisdom. Wisdom is the key quality of the sacral chakra.

Why You Lose Touch With Your Soul's Wisdom

I recently read a quote by Lao Tzu: "If you are depressed, you are living in the past. If you are anxious, you are living in the future. If you are at peace, you are living in the present." This is true. Dwelling on the past reminds us of our regrets or of abusive situations we've been in, which can result in depression. When we think about all the what-ifs of the future, we are often filled with fear and worry and become anxious. It's only when we let go of past regrets and stop anticipating tomorrow's problems that we can be fully in this moment.

Living in this moment—the here and now—is where we find stillness. Being still is where we get in touch with the essence of our soul, our wisdom.

Have You Lost Touch with Your Inner Wisdom?

A few signs you may be out of touch with your inner wisdom include:

* ❋ You're stuck in a job you hate.
* ❋ You're in relationships that pull you down.
* ❋ You have no creative outlet.
* ❋ You have feelings of apathy, meaning you've given up on having a purpose-filled work life or meaningful relationships, or ever painting that masterpiece or writing that book.

The reason a painter loses all sense of time while painting and a musician composes late into the night is that to the soul, every moment is infinite—timeless. And when we create relationships that celebrate our uniqueness, we honor that same deep knowing. We dance to the rhythms of life with abandon. Passions ignite as talents come to life, awakening our soul and shaping our surroundings.

But when we stop doing things that feed our urge to express ourselves creatively, we lose our sense of joy. Joy happens when you lose all track of time while doing something your soul loves, like the painter, writer, or musician. Deep feelings of joy exist in the place where you bliss out. Connecting with your joy, your bliss, through creative action, is a direct path to your higher, wiser soul self.

"Every child is an artist. The problem is how to remain an artist once we grow up."

—Pablo Picasso

Ways to Reconnect with the Wisdom of Your Soul

1) Try Something New. If you don't know what your talents or skills are, or have lost touch with your sense of purpose, seek out volunteer opportunities. Pay attention to the activities that leave you feeling alive! Sometimes volunteering opens ideas and opportunities for career changes that you might not have otherwise considered.

2) Move Your Body. Swimming (outside if possible) is one of the best physical actions for the second chakra for two reasons: 1) the water element is associated with the sacral chakra; and 2) swimming allows your hips (the location of the sacral chakra) to move freely from side to side as you reach and pull with each stroke, releasing tension and blocked energy. Some other ideas to open the hips are forward, backward, and side-angle bends in yoga; belly dancing; and Hula-Hooping!

3) Journal Each Morning, First Thing! Julia Cameron's book *The Artist's Way* offers guidance on writing what she

calls "morning pages." The process works to help you dis-
cover talents and rejuvenate your creativity. After a week
or two, read what you've written. Notice patterns or hints
of secret desires. Have you always wanted to play the guitar
or sing? Did you use to paint but stopped? After reviewing
your writing, sit in stillness, in meditation, for just a bit. Be
quiet and listen.

4) Be Here Now. I like to say, "While peeling potatoes,
peel potatoes." Being mindful of your every action within
the most basic tasks helps to develop the habit of being in
touch with your feelings. Over time, you'll naturally begin
to rely on your feelings as truth. Truth is the path to your
inner knowing.

5) Embrace Your Creativity. Don't let anybody ever con-
vince you that you are not creative—and if you hold the be-
lief that you are not worthy of sharing your creative talents,
let it go. It's simply not true. You were born an intuitive,
creative, joyful being. Avoid anyone who says otherwise.

6) Say Daily Affirmations. Affirm every day, "I am an important, creative, wise soul."

How Will You Know You Are Following Your Wisdom?

When guided by your soul's wisdom, you are deeply connected to the positive aspects associated with the second chakra. You are naturally more creative and playful. Your attitude is more flexible and you are intuitive. You feel great appreciation for the simplest pleasures in life. You are free-flowing and open to change. You know what your purpose is, or you're on the path to discovering it. You are no longer guided by the past but embracing the pull, the potential, found in the here and now.

Chapter 4
Power

The third of the seven major chakras running along the spine is the lumbar chakra, located near the navel and solar plexus. The third chakra is about power—personal power—and it is associated with the fire element. Engaging third chakra fire energy ignites will and determination while promoting positive qualities like self-trust, self-respect, self-love, self-confidence, enthusiasm, and courage. Allowing your fire to smolder, on the other hand, promotes negative traits like self-pity, low self-esteem, victim mentality, self-doubt, and self-judgment. Negative traits like these are paralyzing because they disconnect us from our inner knowing—the ability to trust our gut. Feeling indecisive, confused, frustrated, and even angry makes you stuck. A strong sense of self—personal power—is essential for tuning into your inner wisdom and developing intuition.

Why You Lose Your Personal Power

Falling into the victim role is the main way we lose power. When you fall into the victim mentality, you stop trusting yourself and allow others to choose for you. When you feel disempowered, you attract other power-suckers into your life. Here are some common scenarios that rob energy from the third chakra:

* Saying yes when you mean no.
* Living a cluttered life full of piles of things waiting to be filed, read, paid, and responded to.
* Blaming others or complaining about their impact on you and/or your unhappiness.
* Indecision and second-guessing yourself because you no longer have faith in your own instincts or ability to trust your gut.
* Self-sabotaging by not "showing up" and honoring commitments you've made to yourself or others.
* Comparing yourself to others, which results in developing an attitude of "what's the point"—making you lose motivation and even stop loving yourself.

Because of its location in the gut, blocked energy in the third chakra can cause illness related to the stomach, pancreas, gallbladder, liver, and lumbar spine. Depression, lack of confidence, eating disorders, or feeling overly sensitive to the behaviors of others also indicates a deficient third chakra.

How to Reclaim Your Power

Self-confidence is not about what you have—fancy titles, cars, or large salary—but knowing that you can show up for yourself. Self-confidence is trusting yourself to move your life in a positive direction. Self-confidence is drawing on that inner fire to do whatever it takes even when—especially when—you don't feel like it! When you trust yourself to do the best you can with what you have in any given moment, that's confidence. Here are a few tools to build self-confidence:

1) Take Personal Responsibility. Other people's actions can make you feel like the victim—powerless. But it's not their behavior that puts you in the role of victim; it's how you react that steals your power. Stop blaming others or expecting them to behave a certain way. What others do, don't do, say, or don't say is not about you!

2) De-clutter—Inside and Out. Having a desk so full you can't see the surface blocks creativity and sucks enthusiasm from your space. Or maybe it's your computer desktop, refrigerator, closet, car, garage—or all of the above—that's too messy. Clearing out clutter is kindling for the soul; it sets you on fire! Engage a friend to get you motivated, or, if it's in the budget, hire a professional organizer or feng shui consultant.

3) Push Your Limits. As paralympics athlete and bilateral amputee Aimee Mullins says, "Until we're tested we don't know what we're made of." Maybe you've wanted try rock climbing, swimming, kickboxing, dancing, a triathlon, or something else that feels out of reach. Do something to test your mental and physical limits. Regardless of the outcome, the mere act of "going for it" takes courage—and courage builds confidence.

4) Know Thyself. Get to know your strengths and weaknesses by taking a personality or enneagram test. Study people who inspire you. Even pay attention to who or what irritates you. All feedback is an opportunity to get to know yourself on a deeper level. Self-awareness is power! As Abraham Lincoln said, "I don't think much of a man who is not wiser today than he was yesterday."

5) Trust Your Gut. Keep an Intuition Journal. Track intuitive hits, vibes, feelings, and dreams. Recall times when you wish you'd listened to your gut. What would be different if you had? Follow gut feelings and journal about the outcomes.

6) Sun Salutations. The third chakra is your internal sun! Sun salutations involve a flow of several yoga poses. Seek out a yoga teacher or look online for a routine; the practice is physically stimulating, and it awakens your inner fire! Do several rounds each morning (facing east if possible).

7) Do It Anyway. The only way to bust through fear is to sweat bullets and do it anyway! Choose one small thing you tend to resist—like making the bed—and do it every day for a month. Feel victorious for conquering the dread and doing it anyway! Exaggerate your enthusiasm! Feel it! Apply this triumphant feeling of success as you imagine doing something harder, like public speaking or taking on a leadership role. Make a list of your accomplishments—big and small—and review it often. Give yourself three atta girls/boys every day!

What Does It Feel Like When You're in Your Power Place?

Being in your power place is about owning your personal power and accepting and celebrating you—all of you! It's hearing your own voice and smiling. It's looking in the mirror and loving what you see. It's living in alignment with your inner wisdom while claiming your place in this world. It's about believing in you!

> *"Life is like riding a bicycle—in order to keep your balance, you must keep moving."*
>
> —Albert Einstein

Chapter 5
Love

The fourth of the seven chakras, called the heart chakra, is located in the chest and the area around the thoracic spine. The heart chakra's key quality is love, and it is associated with the air element. To love openly and unconditionally is like merging love and air. Air is expansive, soft, gentle. It's invisible, and yet we know when it's there. Same with love. You just know it when you feel it—in your heart.

Sharing love's tenderness is like a soft wind. The positive qualities of the heart—compassion, understanding, forgiveness—become like wildflowers, blossoming in the most unlikely places. Having a closed heart, on the other hand, allows the weeds of negativity to take root and smother the seeds of love.

The heart chakra is a bridge between the lower, physically-oriented chakras, and the higher, spiritually centered chakras. Only through embracing the meaning of unconditional love may we ascend into higher states of consciousness.

What Blocks Energy in The Heart Chakra

Energy in the heart center is primarily blocked for three reasons: 1) resentment or bitterness with an unwillingness to forgive past grievances; 2) loving others with conditions or attachment to outcome; or 3) being overly empathetic— meaning you take on another person's pain and suffering.

> *"As I walked out the door toward the gate*
> *that would lead to my freedom, I knew if I*
> *didn't leave my bitterness and hatred behind,*
> *I'd still be in prison."*
>
> —*Nelson Mandela*

The heart chakra is associated with the heart, lungs, breasts, circulatory system, ribs, arms, thoracic spine, and thymus gland. The thymus gland is the master gland of the immune system. Because autoimmune disease involves the body attacking itself, working with the heart chakra (self-love), along with the lumbar chakra (located in the navel/ solar plexus area and related to how you tend to your own personal needs) is both logical and necessary for healing autoimmune-related issues.

How to Balance the Heart Chakra

Love is the answer to all suffering. Especially self-love. Loving yourself is not selfish. In fact, loving yourself without condition is fundamental in developing unconditionally loving relationships with others. Here are some actions that promote unconditional love:

1) **Hugging.** When hugging someone, place your hands at the back of their heart center, right between the shoulder blades. Imagine love flowing from your heart—through your hands—into the heart of that person. Hold for seven seconds!

2) **Integrated Self-Love.** To love yourself simply means to take good care of your body, mind, and spirit—equally. Consume things to help your body thrive. Have a positive and loving attitude. Explore and nurture what has meaning in your life. Total integration of mind-body-spirit equals balanced emotions—and a happy heart!

3) Random Acts of Kindness. Doing nice things for others refuels the heart. Not telling anyone (especially the recipient) about the act is even better. Keeping it a secret will make your heart swell with love every time you see that person.

4) Letting Go. To let go means to surrender. To surrender past grievances is to forgive. As Nelson Mandela said, "Resentment is like drinking poison and then hoping it will kill your enemies." Forgiving heals the heart and releases resentment, allowing space for love to spring anew.

5) Just For Today. In the practice of Reiki there are five principles practitioners are expected to honor and teach. Each principle begins with "Just for today . . ." Try applying a "just for today" mentality to shift your attitude or change a habit. For example, "Just for today, I will practice non-judgment," or "Just for today, I will honor my body."

6) Laughing. A good, hearty laugh is so good for our health that we now have professional "laugh therapists" to induce laughing! Laughing reduces stress, depression, and anxiety and benefits the immune, cardiovascular, and respiratory systems. Seek out a Laugh Therapy class, rent some funny movies, or go to a comedy club with friends. And be sure to laugh out loud!

7) Heart-Opening Yoga Postures. Backbends and forward bends are perfect for opening the front as well as back of the heart chakra. "Lead with the heart" is a common instruction used to guide students into these poses. Try "leading with your heart" outside of yoga class. Keep loving thoughts at the center of all your interactions.

8) Tapping on Your Heart Center. Tapping on the chest awakens energy to support cardiovascular and immune system function. Tapping is also a quick remedy to encourage deep breathing in stressful situations. Find an EFT (Emotional Freedom Technique) practitioner to learn specifics. Or connect with the Tarzan within and beat to your own rhythm!

9) Neutrality. In yoga we work to achieve a "neutral" spine so energy can freely move up "the river of life" (the spine) with minimal effort. Taking a neutral position with others is the same because it develops objectivity. Through understanding we find compassion. Listening without judgment allows you to protect your heart while being fully present for others.

10) Karma Yoga. Devoting oneself to being in service to others without expectation of reward—volunteering eagerly and happily with the best intentions—is karma yoga.

Ah, but there is a reward! It isn't possible to help someone and not feel genuine love in your heart.

11) Breathing. Science has proven that proper breathing improves overall health and wellness. Take a meditation or yoga class and learn the Ujjayi breath, which utilizes the full capacity of the lungs. The Ujjayi breath is very oxygenating, circulates prana throughout your whole being, and benefits the entire cardiorespiratory system. It is both meditative and rejuvenating!

What Does Unconditional Love Feel Like?

To know true love is to know God. To know God is to know yourself. The ultimate devotional act to God is self-love. To Know Thyself completely, tenderly accepting all of what you see, then sharing that which you know by being that which you are—this is unconditional love.

Chapter 6

Calmness

The fifth of the seven major chakras running along the spine is the throat chakra, located in the area around the cervical spine. The phrase "speak your truth" is commonly associated with the throat chakra. This phrase may have been best captured by Joseph Campbell, who also coined another phrase: "Follow your bliss." Following your bliss is living in alignment with your purpose, your truth.

Naturally, because of its location, how we communicate has a direct influence on the throat chakra. Negative words and tones are harmful to the throat chakra. Using thoughtful words and listening with an empathetic ear—to your wise self as well as others—enhances the energy of the throat chakra and clears the path toward bliss!

Common Bliss Busters

Three specific behaviors block energy in the throat chakra more than anything else. I call these behaviors Bliss Busters! They limit your potential to ever truly experience the sense of ease and calm that comes from living in alignment with your deepest purpose (where you feel bliss). Some common Bliss Busters are:

> ❋ **Gossiping.** Talking about others is one of the biggest assaults to the throat chakra.
>
> ❋ **Complaining.** Whining, nagging, judging, and grumbling are toxic and block positive energy (people and situations) from entering your life.
>
> ❋ **Blaming.** Faulting others is judging and not taking personal responsibility to help find a positive solution.

When you stop gossiping, complaining, and blaming, it's like unclogging a plugged-up drain. The path is cleared for energy to move in and keep the throat free-flowing and open.

Because it's located in the neck, fifth chakra issues show up related to the thyroid, esophagus, jaw, mouth, gums, teeth, and to limited mobility in the cervical spine.

An overactive throat chakra shows up as being too talkative, interrupting, or having an overbearing tone.

Clearing the Path To Bliss

Letting go of bad habits, then replacing them with positive behaviors, is how we clear the path in our pursuit of bliss. What follows are a few suggestions to root out the bad energy and make room for the good!

1) Do a 10-Day Detox. Avoid negative words, thoughts, judgments, complaining, gossiping, and criticizing for the next ten days. Don't complain about a single thing or person. As a bonus, make a list of positive attributes about anyone who bugs you. Find at least five things!

2) Improve Your Communication Skills. Attend a class to learn effective communication. Nonviolent Communication (NVC) teaches "empathic listening" and "compassionate communication" using an easy-to-apply set of guidelines. The mere act of listening with compassion or empathy releases blame, judgment, and the temptation to gossip (those top three Bliss Busters). What we say, how we say it, and when we say it has a major influence on our throat chakra.

3) Study Animal Energy. In Ted Andrew's book, *Animal Speak*, he writes about how giraffe energy has to do with communication and being farsighted. NVC also uses the giraffe as a metaphor for effective communication. Sticking your neck out to "speak your truth," without losing sight of the need to look ahead at the consequences (being farsighted), gets you one step closer to truth—to bliss. The giraffe also teaches us to listen from the heart, with empathy, because it is the land animal with the largest heart. Pay attention if the giraffe shows up in your life. Chances are something related to communication needs attention.

4) Use a Talking Stick. A talking stick is a way to give each member of a group an opportunity to speak and to keep the conversation moving. The stick is passed around, giving the person holding it an invitation to speak without interruption. Only the person holding the stick is allowed to speak. Setting a time limit and sitting in a circle is best.

5) Put a Cork in It. Use a cork from a wine bottle to prop open your mouth and give your jaw muscles a break. No kidding! Place the cork vertically between your front teeth. Relax your jaw. Close your eyes. Relax the muscles along either side of your face. Allow each exhalation to serve as a prompt for deeper relaxation. Inhale. Exhale, releasing tension around your ears, neck, and entire face. Feel the expansion deep in your throat as you breathe. (Tip: Cut the cork to a length that's best for you.)

6) Try Public Speaking. Even if you don't intend to speak publicly, the practice will help you develop confidence in articulating your feelings (where purpose and bliss hide!). The process of writing and giving speeches in a safe and supportive environment helps uncover tidbits of "truth" waiting to be told. Try Toastmasters or the National Speaker's Association.

7) Practice Yoga. Inversions are good for the throat chakra, especially poses that elongate the neck. Try Bridge, Fish, or Plow Pose. Certain poses can cause serious injury to the cervical spine and neck without the use of props to ensure proper alignment, so make sure to seek out a qualified yoga teacher.

8) Say I Love You—A Lot. That's it.

How Do You Know You're Following Your Bliss?

It's not necessarily easy to figure out your calling—your bliss—let alone to follow it. Poet and philosopher Mark Nepo teaches that "holding nothing back" is how we come to know what we are truly capable of. Holding nothing back is listening to your heart and letting it lead you. When you do, every move is fueled by love. Just as the stem of a rose pulls nutrients from the earth, so too does your heart give rise to your voice, your truth, when you step into a life fueled by love—and, like the rose, you expand and bloom.

In speaking your truth, you become like the fully blossomed rose: radiant, poised and calm—basking in the light, just doing what you do. This is bliss.

> *"Follow your bliss and the universe will open doors for you where there were only walls."*
>
> —*Joseph Campbell*

Chapter 7
Light and Sound

The sixth of the seven major chakras is commonly referred to as the third eye because its positive pole is located at the point between the eyebrows. Its negative pole is located in the back of the head, at the medulla oblongata (base of the skull)—the entry point of prana, or life force energy.

There are two key aspects associated with the sixth chakra: light, as in *seeing the light;* and sound, as in *listening to your inner voice.* The sixth chakra is related to being clairvoyant or psychic. This is the chakra that's most deeply connected with the "sixth sense" or intuition.

Intuitive Inhibitors

Although some people are simply born more intuitive than others, everyone has the capacity to cultivate intuition. Regardless of where we fall on the intuitive scale, sustaining a constant connection to your inner guidance system is a challenge for everyone, and the main culprit for losing touch is stress.

Stress comes in many forms, but it always throws you into survival mode. In survival mode, thoughts and actions are fear-based, resulting in confusion, indecisiveness, and loads of stress. Instead of being in a receptive mode—seeing and listening for guidance—you're on alert, guarded, ready to be attacked, ready to defend.

Imbalances in the sixth chakra result in migraines, eyes problems, brain fog, hallucinations, nightmares, poor concentration, hearing problems, and tunnel vision (narrow-mindedness).

Developing Intuition

Intuition is the language of the soul. It comes in gently, like a whisper, and often randomly, in the way of epiphanies or lightbulb moments. As naturally as you draw on your other senses to enhance day-to-day living, with practice you will come to rely on and expect intuitive guidance and more of those "aha" moments. Over time, you can even create an "on demand" sixth sense. Below are a few tips for strengthening intuition:

1) **Keep Your (Third) Eye on the Prize.** Meditating at the third eye magnetizes energy to the prefrontal lobe of the brain—the area that governs creativity and concentration—as well as the pineal and pituitary glands, which produce stress-combating hormones. Focusing at the point between the eyebrows also enhances creative visualization exercises, the practice of holding a clear image of an intended desire in your mind's eye while introducing affirmations. The rewards for focusing on the third eye are infinite!

2) **Cool Your Engines.** When we're stressed, we literally overheat. Our bodies get inflamed and suffer illness. We become "hotheaded" and emotionally spent. The Sitali, or the cooling breath, is especially good for "chilling out" during stressful times. It helps to avoid overheating your system. Begin by curling your tongue like a straw and sticking it out between your lips just a bit. Inhale through your mouth (and through your curled tongue). It should feel cool. As you inhale, tilt your head back and imagine energy flowing into the back of the sixth chakra (the medulla oblongata). Close your mouth and eyes. Pause. Now, gently draw your head back to center, chin parallel to the floor, exhaling through your nose. Practice for up to five minutes.

3) **Massage Your Medulla.** Massaging the back of the sixth chakra at the medulla oblongata while focusing

on the point between the eyebrows increases the flow of energy. Using your fingertips, reach back and apply a little pressure. Close your eyes. Inhale as you rub to the right several times. Exhale and rub to the left the same number of times as you did on the right. This left/right motion induces the natural up-and-down flow of energy in the spine—circulating up as you inhale, circulating down as you exhale. Tip: Combine with the "cooling breath" for an even greater flow of energy.

4) **Divination Tools.** Tarot and angel cards, animal and nature totems, runes, pendulums, and colors are all examples of divination tools. Experiment with a variety of tools. It doesn't matter which one you're drawn to. Study the meaning behind any given tool and give it a chance to develop as a primary source of communication. Once the Universe knows your favorite method of communication, you can expect more messages to flow in using that particular process.

5) **Exercise Your Abilities.** Just like a muscle that atrophies when not used, your guiding light grows dim when unattended to. Your wise inner voice grows weak when ignored. Trusting your vibes as a matter of course is as necessary for building intuition as eating good food and moving your body is to keeping physically healthy. The more you rely on (use) your inner guidance system, the more refined, strong,

and accurate your intuitive abilities become. Focusing on the third eye during physical activity increases the flow of energy too. While running, walking, skiing, hiking, or doing yoga, practice holding your chin up and keeping your eyes looking up and forward.

What's it Like to be Guided by Intuition?

Intuitive people are often thought of as "lucky" or living a charmed life. It's true to a point, but what is luck? The truth is that *luck* doesn't necessarily come easy—not at first, anyway. Ironically, it's often through suffering or great effort that we learn to slow down enough to examine why life isn't easy. It's through this slowing-down process that intuition (luck) sneaks in.

When guided by intuition, your surroundings are more vibrant. You feel creative, confident, and empowered to speak your truth; you feel loving, grounded, and at peace. Basically, your entire energy system is alive and thriving. Tapping into your intuition keeps you firing on all cylinders, so to speak.

As you navigate life guided by your soul, you appear to have it so easy, when all you're doing is going with the flow—adjusting your sails to catch the breeze, listening to the voice of your inner, wiser soul self.

"*Your vision will become clear only when you look into your heart. Who looks outside, dreams. Who looks inside, awakens.*"

—Carl Gustav Jung

Chapter 8
Bliss

The seventh and final major chakra is located at the top of the head and, because of its location, is called the crown chakra. The crown chakra serves as a channel, or a pathway, for shifting us from human consciousness to divine consciousness. Spirituality is associated with the seventh chakra. It's where we merge with the essence of Godlike energy. It is considered "the seat of the soul."

The crown chakra's key aspect is bliss—the ultimate state of joy. Bliss is experienced in the non-dualistic state of higher awareness, when our human consciousness and soul consciousness are no longer in opposition but joined by loving, divine energy. Deeper states of consciousness are sometimes described as "blissing out" or having an out-of-body experience. It's a natural high. No longer limited or bound by the physical body, you are free.

We lack bliss when we are disconnected from spirit. Instead of feeling liberated we feel incomplete, limited, like something important is missing. That's because, as so beautifully stated by philosopher and priest Pierre Teilhard de Chardin, "We are spiritual beings having a human experience." It's simply unnatural to live a life devoid of spirit.

Symptoms of Spiritual Separation

Signs of a spiritual separation include: (1) your existence feels pointless, dull, empty, or lacking direction, meaning, or purpose; (2) you question the existence of, or no longer trust in, a higher power; (3) you feel an impending sense of doom, perhaps like you might even die, or that everything is falling apart.

Seventh chakra imbalances present as skin disorders, apathy, vertigo, confusion, anxiety, depression, distrust, and paranoia. From an energy medicine point of view, when these subtler signs are ignored, life-altering events such as nervous breakdowns, life-threatening illnesses, serious accidents, or near-death experiences show up, quite literally bringing you to your knees.

Reconnecting to Spirit

Getting down on your knees, so to speak, is the most direct path to Spirit. How you get there—to your knees—does not necessarily require going through a major life event. But what you do once you're on your knees makes all the difference in your results. Below are some suggestions for reconnecting with spirit.

1) **Praying.** Prayer is for honoring God, but it's also where we go for guidance and help, and to resolve problems. Regardless of your reason, always begin prayer in a state of appreciation. Counting your blessings sets the tone to one that most resembles Godlike energy. Next, repeat "Thank you for loving me" for several minutes. Tune into the moment. My mom taught me that when it comes to asking for help, "Don't talk to God about your problems, talk to your problems about God." Consider a current problem. How would you share your knowledge of God with the problem? How could your understanding of God help? What would you say? Instead of simply "turning it over to God," shift your circumstances by consciously and deliberately sharing your wisdom. Set the scene and watch it play out. Observe the outcome. Close by giving thanks to God for helping you and for loving you.

2) **Seclusion.** One day a week or month, retreat into silence. Avoid communication with others. Eat small amounts of

high-energy foods (fruits and vegetables, or try a juice fast). Drink plenty of water. Bless everything you consume. Enjoy meditation, yoga, inspirational reading, and nature walks. Watch the grass grow, bark stretch, leaves dance, birds soar, and clouds float. Feel the earth move. See what's before you. Feel what's inside you. Delight in yourself during this spiritual cleanse.

3) Sacred Spaces. The divine energy in sacred places (temples, churches, synagogues) is palpable, luring us to visit and stay awhile. Cultivate something similar in your meditation or prayer space at home by practicing in the same spot. As the spiritual vibration increases, you'll be called to sit more often. Get a bench or cushion; use a blanket or shawl. Include rocks, minerals, mementos, candles, photographs of loved ones or deities—whatever makes you feel joyful. Burn incense to clear negative energy while inviting in spiritually charged energy (moldavite-infused sticks are an excellent choice). Create a comfortable, inspirational space.

4) Spinal Sweep. Humming or chanting aum (om) at each chakra "sweeps" away blockages while inducing vital life force energy to move up the spine. Place your hands on or near each of the seven major chakras while using your voice to "om" (or hum). Start with the first chakra and work your way up. Here's a reminder regarding locations: chakra

1: base of the pelvic floor; chakra 2: a few inches above the pubic bone; chakra 3: navel/solar plexus; chakra 4: chest/heart center; chakra 5: throat/neck; chakra 6: middle of brow/third eye; chakra 7: crown. Don't control the energy. Relax into it. As the great yogi Paramhansa Yogananda said, "Aum is the bridge between human consciousness and cosmic consciousness." If you're not feeling anything, don't worry, it'll come. Sometimes there's just more sweeping to do. Keep at it.

The Power of Bliss

Not only is bliss found in prayer and meditation, but in small increments of time waiting to be embraced—tasted, smelled, touched, seen, and heard. It's not somewhere else, it's right where you're planted. It's inside you. Meditation and prayer teach us how to still the mind as a matter of habit so we don't overlook bliss as we go about living.

Bliss is in the air, the rain, flowers, mountain peaks, the ocean's roar. It's a child's laugh, rollercoaster rides, high dives, hang gliding, and open-water swims. It's a few words of prose, the rhythm of song, a brush filled with paint. It's where things fall together instead of apart. Bliss is the very elegance of nature simply taking its course. All we have to do is let it.

"You don't have to walk on your knees for a hundred miles through the desert, repenting. You only have to let the soft animal of your body love what it loves."

—Mary Oliver

Chapter 9
Trinity of Truth

When we live in balance with mind, body, and spirit, life flows more naturally, more easily. This harmonious state is what I call the Trinity of Truth. The Trinity is comprised of the three components of your Being—mind, body, spirit— and the Truth is your commitment to live in alignment with your soul—your purpose.

Each element of the Trinity of Truth is connected to various aspects of your energy body by way of a particular energy center. The connection between mind-body-spirit and the energy body provides guidance when we learn to tune in and pay attention to how we react in any given situation. A simple example of how this connection works is something that is experienced by all of us when we get cut off in traffic. Your first reaction may be to get mad and perhaps even yell, even though the person who cut you off can't hear you! Your emotional reaction only hurts you by disrupting your personal energy; first in your mind, then in your body. Your mental state has gone from peacefully going about your day to feeling angry. Your breathing shortens and your throat tightens, and those mental and physical reactions affect particular energy centers. Your throat, heart, and lumbar chakras take a direct hit.

The great yogi Paramhansa Yogananda teaches in his book *Scientific Healing Affirmations* that:

> *"In his mortal aspect man is a Triune Being. He longs for freedom from all varieties of suffering. His needs are: (1) Healing of bodily diseases. (2) Healing of mental or psychological diseases . . . (3) Healing of spiritual diseases . . ."*

Yogananda also teaches the importance of giving equal attention to all three aspects of your being—your Trinity—in order to prevent and cure disease in all areas of your life.

The Mind-Body-Spirit (MBS) Scan

The mind-body-spirit scan serves as a Trinity of Truth check-in and begins with three simple questions: (1) Am I having good thoughts and a positive attitude (mind)?; (2) Am I consuming things that are good for me and getting plenty of rest and exercise (body)?; and (3) Have I been meditating (or engaging in another practice) to support my spiritual health (spirit)? Generally you'll find that all three—mind, body, and spirit—are being neglected to some degree, but most often one of the three more than the other two. Knowing which element of the Trinity of Truth is most out of alignment gives you a starting place from which to choose an action to correct an imbalance.

Let's try it:
Close your eyes. Take a few deep, cleansing breaths to get centered. Relax into your body as you inhale. Exhale tension. Feeling grounded and centered, ask some questions related to mind, body, and spirit.

Sample questions:
Mind: Do I have a negative or positive attitude right now? Am I feeling depressed, anxious, sensitive, or angry? Am I holding a grudge or resentment? Am I working toward having only positive thoughts?

▶ **Body:** Am I eating and drinking things that make my body thrive? Am I moving my body at least a little bit every day, or am I sitting around too much?

Spirit: When is the last time I sat in silence, went for a nature walk, prayed, or meditated? What one creative act brings me joy, and when is the last time I did it? Do I connect with myself as a spiritual being?

Consider what area feels the most out of balance and what one small thing you can do to propel yourself forward positively, balancing mind, body, and spirit. If it's not apparent after answering these questions, try journaling a few pages to help gain clarity.

The Awareness-Action-Affirmation (AAA) Plan

Another simple tool to use after gaining clarity is what I call the AAA Plan. Think of it as a three-step action plan. The first step is Awareness, which can be accomplished through any introspective activity, such as the MBS Scan. The second step is to choose an Action. The third step is writing the Affirmation.

Let's try it:

Examine the results of your MBS scan. What is being neglected? Maybe it's a simple attitude (mental) adjustment that's needed. Maybe you've been expecting your partner to be a better listener, but instead of talking to him or her about it, you hold thoughts like, *Why can't he/she at least pretend to be listening to me?!*—which only adds to your annoyance and negative feelings. To counteract your (negative) automatic response, an affirmation might go something like this: "I have only positive thoughts, hold no judgments, release all expectations of others, and live in this moment—*my* moment—here and now."

Write a sentence or two for each step: Awareness, Action, and Affirmation. Just like you carry jumper cables, proof of insurance, and perhaps even your AAA membership card in case your car breaks down and needs towing, carry this AAA Plan—your three-step action plan—to help you stay balanced as you navigate daily life. Keep it close at hand and refer to it often. Review it when you feel tempted to veer off course by taking something personally, feel offended by the behaviors of others, lack confidence, or simply feel out of sorts and you don't know why.

How the MBS Scan and AAA Plan Balance the Chakras

The MBS Scan identifies imbalances in the Trinity, giving you something to work with. The AAA Plan serves as a reminder of what you've decided to do with the "something" that's throwing you off. Taking any action to balance mind, body, and spirit automatically improves the overall health of the energy centers because of the ripple effect; that is to say, one positive action leads to another positive action. Since the chakras are connected to the eight aspects of God—peace, wisdom, power, love, calmness, light, sound, and bliss—you can't help but experience a deeper sense of health and harmony when you focus on achieving balance between mind, body, and spirit.

Chapter 10

Affirmations For The Chakras

The body's energy centers hold both negative and positive energy. How each one expresses itself—more positively or more negatively—changes from moment to moment, day to day, and week to week. It all depends on what's going on in your life and how you're handling it.

In order to reach our maximum potential, we have to clear out any negative energy. It's like managing weeds in a garden. An overlooked weed grows deep roots and competes with what you've planted. Sometimes you're too busy to see the weed; you may even walk right past it without noticing it's there. Other times you might actually notice the weed, but instead of pulling it right then, you put it off for another day. Next thing you know, the rains come and the weeds have multiplied.

Making a conscious effort to see a negative trait in yourself, then working to clear it, is akin to seeking out the weed in your garden and pulling it. It clears the path for more goodness to grow in your life—especially knowing that the rains will always come.

Using the Negative to Affirm the Positive

Exploring negative feelings to their fullest serves as a launch pad to propel you deeper into the opposing positive quality. For example, feeling the pain of sadness helps you feel the sweetness of joy. Without darkness you cannot know light.

A good way to overpower negativity is to be with the negative feelings, to feel them completely, and then to immediately plant a seed of the opposite—positive—energy in its place. Using affirmations is a simple and effective way to do this. To affirm something is to state it as if it is so, here and now. It is to declare something as if it is already true; to believe it is real.

Below are the three most common negative traits (weeds) related to each chakra, followed by an opposing positive (seed) in the form of an affirmation.

Chakra 1: rigid, unstable, unsafe. Affirmation: "Knowing that life will hold me, protect me, and nurture me, I am safe and at peace."

Chakra 2: addictive, flighty, stuck. Affirmation: "I am a wise, free-flowing, creative, and whole being."

Chakra 3: judgmental, insecure, controlling. Affirmation: "Knowing that I am a perfect, powerful expression of God, I celebrate others in their unique expression of God."

Chakra 4: resentful, jealous, rescuer. Affirmation: "I love and respect others unconditionally because I love myself without conditions."

Chakra 5: blaming, gossipy, pessimistic. Affirmation: "Because I know we're all connected, I speak of others with a calming sense of love and grace."

Chakra 6: indecisive, egotistical, confused. Affirmation: "Seeing and hearing clearly, I humbly trust my intuition."

Chakra 7: lost, apathetic, depressed. Affirmation: "Vital life force energy runs through my veins. I am Spirit, I am bliss!"

Tackling a negative thought with will and determination—like you mean it—and then examining all sides of it helps in creating positive, meaningful, and *relevant* affirmations.

Feeling Feeds the Words

You can say words all day long, but if they lack meaning they are missing essential energy; they have no power. Think of the essence of any given word. What does love feel like? Or anger, or sadness, or joy, or peace? Pause to "feel" a word's meaning, its expression.

Feeling gives meaning to words just as water cultivates growth in a garden. Words fueled by feeling become like a well-tended garden soaking up a warm summer's rain. The water releases vital nutrients from the soil that feed the plants just as feeling releases the essence, the nutrient, of a word. Feeling is what makes the affirmation come to life, makes it take root and grow.

Chakra-Clearing Chant

The chakra-clearing chant is an affirming exercise to cleanse the entire chakra system in one fell swoop or as a single affirmation or mantra. To begin, close your eyes and take a few deep, cleansing breaths. Get centered. Be still. Invite energy to flow upward with each inhalation and down with each exhalation as you say the words. Keep your gaze uplifted. Practice outside or near a window if you can.

I am pure, I am free
Grounded like a tree!

I am pure, I am free
To express creatively!

I am pure, I am free
Accepting all of me!

I am pure, I am free
Love embraces me!

I am pure, I am free
Speaking joyfully!

I am pure, I am free
With clarity I see!

I am pure, I am free
As I unite with Thee!

Yes, I am pure, I am free . . . I live authentically!

For the last statement, tilt your head back and lift your gaze as you reach toward the sky with open arms. Really concentrate on the *meaning* of the words and how they make you *feel*.

Why Use Affirmations?

Using affirmations helps us achieve self-mastery, self-leadership, self-control, self-management, and self-realization. They also give us liberation! They're a way of taking responsibility for our personal development and progress in life. We can read books, take classes, and listen to lectures, but without taking action, nothing will make a bit of difference.

Affirming the positive is the action of fertilizing your inner garden. It promotes maximum growth from the inside out. You become like the wise farmer who, having planted a tiny little seed and then nurtured it to harvest, ensures further growth by sharing his bountiful crop with others.

> *"The creation of a thousand forests is in one acorn."*
>
> —*Ralph Waldo Emerson*

Chapter 11

Soul-utions

When we do our part to live life according to the eight aspects of God—peace, wisdom, power, love, calmness, light, sound, and bliss—the response from the Universe (God) is reciprocal. That is to say, the level of effort we put into changing our lives for the better is matched in like. If we put out a little effort, the message to the Universe is that we want a little in return. If, on the other hand, we put our hearts into everything we do, meaning a full effort, we are showered with blessings that support our mission, our change.

Change

Oftentimes we let change itself get in the way of our progress toward a more blissful life. This happens because we work harder to change others than to examine ourselves, our own areas in need of positive change. In Michael Jackson's song, "Man in The Mirror," the lyrics say, "If you want to make the world a better place, you better take a look at yourself and make a change . . ." So long as we focus on what's wrong with others, we will never be able to truly see our own need to change. Underneath, in your heart, you might know there's work to do (actually, you know there is!), but to take on that work feels overwhelming. Understandably so.

If you begin by taking little baby steps, the effort will take hold and build momentum. All you have to do is one small thing. Examine your life and notice what aspects are missing and choose one action to address that lack. If you lack a peaceful environment, for example, start clearing out your space—physically and mentally. Take an inventory of who no longer serves you or who feels toxic in your surroundings. Instead of trying to change them, accept them for who they are and turn your focus on your own potential, your own growth.

Expectations and Acceptance

The more you expect others to change, and wait for them to change, the further removed you become from actually ever seeing a change in them because your mind gets so clouded by pent-up emotions and, yes, even more expectations. Frustration sets in, followed by other feelings like resentment, anger, sadness, and despair. You feel victimized by your circumstances. Trying to change others is one area that blocks our potential, but another common area that gets in our way is the unwillingness to accept others for who they are. We hold expectations of others and then can't accept it when they let us down. We work to change them or hold a grievance toward them for being whatever way they are (stupid, insensitive, rude, unkind, or even toxic).

In order to accept someone, we have to let go of expectations and stop judging them. That's not to say we shouldn't expect a coworker to treat us with respect or a child to adhere to our house rules, but when we expect a person's personality or character to be different than it is, we're setting ourselves up for disappointment and frustration. If a person has a sharp tongue and seems to be always itching for a fight, you have to adjust the way you communicate with them. Their behavior, in and of itself, is a form of communication. As long as you can see that, you (being on the high road of self-improvement and positive change) can adopt a different language, so to speak, when you interact with them, and stop hoping or expecting that they'll be different next time you see them.

It's Not About You

The number one thing that keeps you from making a change (or even knowing what change is necessary) is getting trapped in the victim role. Being the victim happens when you take things personally. Taking something personally is thinking that what other people do, don't do, say, or don't say is about you. It's not. A person is going to behave the way they do regardless of who's in their line of fire. It's not about you. Take, for example, the person who, when you give them an inch, takes a mile. They have a pattern of taking advantage of your goodwill. Instead of complaining about it—a victim reaction—tighten your boundaries. It is your responsibility not only to set new boundaries, but to hold them, to prevent being taken advantage of again. It's just a matter of getting to know the people around you and adapting your own behavior and actions to improve the situation. The person who takes and takes and takes is a taker, not a giver. Accept it. Set boundaries. Hold the line.

In many ways, the people who challenge you the most are the best teachers. It's good for us to develop multiple skills around how to communicate. Instead of trying to change someone, look at the relationship as an opportunity for personal growth and learning. Setting boundaries is important, but it only goes so far sometimes. It's especially tough with family members and close friends—people you can only separate from so much, who you either can't or wouldn't really want to divorce from your life altogether. For these people, the ones you truly love and care about, nurturing the relationship can feel one-sided, like you're doing all the nurturing (and you very likely are). In this case, setting boundaries requires a gentle approach and a little more work on your part. And it needs to stem from a loving place.

> *"If we learn to open our hearts, anyone, including the people who drive us crazy, can be our teacher."*
>
> —*Pema Chodron*

Coming to a relationship from a loving place is easier when you understand that "it" (their behavior) is not about you. If someone's behavior irritates you, work on being more patient, observant, interested, or curious about them. Just give them the gift of being there. Nothing more, nothing less. It sounds simple, and it is, but simple is very often far from easy. Just like anything else you want to learn, it just requires a little effort—and, usually, a lot more understanding!

Enrolling The Soul

To recap, the things that get in our way and prevent us from living more closely to the eight aspects of God are not being able or willing to accept "what is" and working hard to change things outside ourselves. Instead, we must work to change what's inside us and let go of falling victim to the actions of others. As we do, we get closer to our true authentic nature, our soul self. When we get in touch with our true nature, we see that everyone is really in the same boat: simply trying to find their way through all the muck— the same as you and me. Understanding this helps ease up the strain to force change, and allows you to accept others as they are. In this more natural, intuitive state of mind, your mind is at peace. When you're at peace, solutions— soul-utions—flow in because you are being guided by an inner knowing. Your soul's knowing; God's knowing. Instead of reacting to an upsetting behavior, you respond from a centered state with a calm presence. Your surroundings can't help but change. You become the change.

You are at the root of all change. If you want more joy in your life, be joyous. If you want more respect, go out of your way to treat others respectfully. If you want more love and affection, be more loving and show others affection. Practice the teachings of Mahatma Gandhi, who so eloquently taught us to "Be the change you wish to see in the world." Simply think of "the world" as your inner self—your sphere of influence. Be whatever it is you wish to see in *that* world; *your* world. Everything else will just fall into place.

"God grant me the serenity to accept the things I cannot change, the courage to change the things I can, and the wisdom to know the difference."

—Reinhold Niebuhr

About the Author

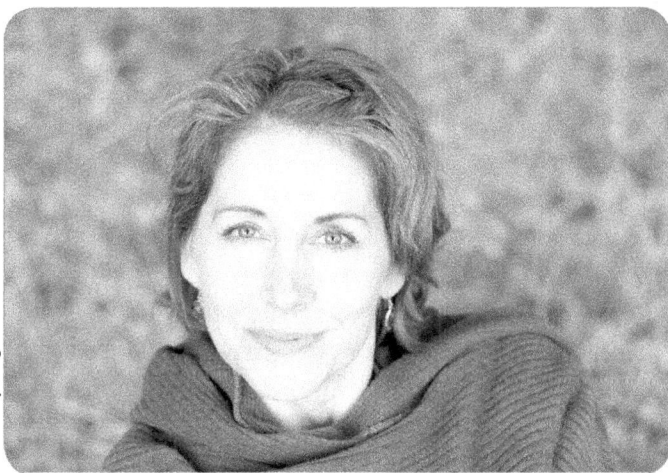

© Misty Carpinito

Ruthie Stender, owner of Seattle Energy Medicine, is a certified meditation teacher and registered yoga instructor with Yoga Alliance. She teaches energy medicine, yoga, and meditation as easy and accessible forms of complementary medicine in her private healing practice, group sessions, and classes. A certified energy medicine practitioner, Reiki master, and business owner, Ruthie mentors others who are pursuing a career in energy healing.

Blending her twenty-three years in aerospace engineering with her current work in the health and wellness industry, Ruthie also offers stress-management classes for the workplace. These courses combine gentle movement and easy-to-learn breathing exercises—making them accessible to everyone.

You can follow Ruthie *@RuthieStender* on Twitter or her Facebook pages, *Seattle Energy Medicine* and *Ruthie Stender, Writer.* Read her blog posts at *www.seattleenergy medicine.com.*

Acknowledgments

First and foremost, I'd like to thank my editor and writing coach, Brooke Warner—one of the most sincere, intuitive, and multi-talented people I know.

Infinite love and gratitude to Bill and Misty for giving me space to practice practicing what I preach while encouraging me to, above everything else I do, keep on writing! And my sweet grandsons, Henry and Oliver, who, by living in the moment, remind me how easy life can be—and how words can just flow—when I pause to do the same.

So much gratitude goes to Krissa Lagos for her help in editing this book. Also huge thanks to Tabitha Lahr for designing a beautiful cover and interior layout. Thank you both for helping me create a book that I love, a book that I am happy to share with others.

I'd also like to thank Krysta Gibson, publisher of New Spirit Journal, for the opportunity to contribute as a monthly columnist. Having a maximum word count and deadline taught me something I'd been lacking as a writer: discipline. Those articles helped me "reset" my goals to shape this very book! Thank you for trusting me to show up every month. And a big thanks to Christy Johnson, who suggested I submit an article in the first place.

Lastly, I'd like to acknowledge Nayaswami Hriman McGilloway for introducing me to the teachings of Paramhansa Yogananda, where I first learned about *the eight aspects of God.*

End Comment by the Author

If you liked *The Eight Aspects of God: A Pathway to Bliss,* you might also enjoy my forthcoming book, *It's Not About You,* which further examines how taking things personally disrupts your overall health and wellness. The book provides a diagnostics tool to determine what's got a hold on you and why you might be taking something personally, along with relevant tools to move you from the victim role toward an achievable proactive role. A book that helps you help yourself, *It's Not About You* will teach you why what other people do, don't do, say, or don't say is not about you; how to avoid falling victim to the behaviors of others in the first place; and how to take charge of your own life!

For a free sampling of the Diagnostics Tool go to my website, www.seattleenergymedicine.com. The Diagnostics works by asking you to rate basic statements made about each of the seven chakras. Once you've rated each of the seven, you will be able to quickly see which (God) aspects are on the low side, needing a little more attention, and which ones are on the high side. Basically, you get to know your strengths and weaknesses with regard to the body's energy system, and your own God aspects. The process is analogous to when I am having problems with my car and take it to the shop. If the issue isn't obvious the mechanic runs a diagnostics to investigate the problem. Depending on the results, he can decide what action is required or if further investigation is needed. Running the diagnostics gives him a starting place, a clue to what might be wrong with the car. The diagnostics found in It's Not About You is just like the mechanic looking for the trouble spot on the car. Once you know which energy center needs your attention, you have something to work with.

The diagnostics exercise is especially helpful when you're feeling stuck and unsure about what the problem is. Oftentimes a client will tell me they just feel indifferent and lack joy but don't know why. They can't pinpoint why they're feeling so blue, and they even feel guilty about it because, on paper, they have nothing to complain about. They have a good-paying job, supportive family, a home, plenty of food, and a comfortable life. It's a common scenario. The thing is, though, you should never feel guilty for being honest about how you really feel. If you lack joy, you lack joy. It is what it is. To find out why is the next step. The diagnostics tool helps to uncover the why and tools like the AAA Plan, as mentioned here in Chapter 9, help with the what to do, as in what to do with the findings.

In gratitude,
Ruthie